LITANY OF HUMILITY

O Jesus! meek and humble of heart,
    ... *Hear me.*
From the desire of being esteemed
    ... *Deliver me, Jesus.*
From the desire of being loved
    ... *Deliver me, Jesus.*
From the desire of being extolled
    ... *Deliver me, Jesus.*
From the desire of being honored
    ... *Deliver me, Jesus.*
From the desire of being praised
    ... *Deliver me, Jesus.*
From the desire of being preferred to others
    ... *Deliver me, Jesus.*
From the desire of being consulted
    ... *Deliver me, Jesus.*
From the desire of being approved
    ... *Deliver me, Jesus.*
From the fear of being humiliated
    ... *Deliver me, Jesus.*
From the fear of being despised
    ... *Deliver me, Jesus.*
From the fear of suffering rebukes
    ... *Deliver me, Jesus.*
From the fear of being calumniated
    ... *Deliver me, Jesus.*
From the fear of being forgotten
    ... *Deliver me, Jesus.*

From the fear of being ridiculed
    ... *Deliver me, Jesus.*
From the fear of being wronged
    ... *Deliver me, Jesus.*
From the fear of being suspected
    ... *Deliver me, Jesus.*

That others may be loved more than I,
    ... *Jesus, grant me the grace to desire it.*
That others may be esteemed more than I
    ... *Jesus, grant me the grace to desire it.*
That, in the opinion of the world, others
may increase and I may decrease,
    ... *Jesus, grant me the grace to desire it.*
That others may be chosen and I set
aside,
    ... *Jesus, grant me the grace to desire it.*
That others may be praised and I unno-
ticed,
    ... *Jesus, grant me the grace to desire it.*
That others may be preferred to me in everything,
    ... *Jesus, grant me the grace to desire it.*
That others may become holier than I,
provided that I may become as holy as I
should,
    ... *Jesus, grant me the grace to desire it.*

    ...Amen

LITANY OF HUMILITY
Prayer and lined journal

Ordering Information:
Quantity sales. Special discounts are available on quantity purchases by corporations, associations, and others. For details visit RoadToPurity.com

COME HOLY SPIRIT, RENEW ME, DWELL IN ME AND PROTECT ME

COME HOLY SPIRIT, RENEW ME, DWELL IN ME AND PROTECT ME

COME HOLY SPIRIT, RENEW ME, DWELL IN ME AND PROTECT ME

COME HOLY SPIRIT, RENEW ME, DWELL IN ME AND PROTECT ME

COME HOLY SPIRIT, RENEW ME, DWELL IN ME AND PROTECT ME

COME HOLY SPIRIT, RENEW ME, DWELL IN ME AND PROTECT ME

COME HOLY SPIRIT, RENEW ME, DWELL IN ME AND PROTECT ME

"To love means loving the unlovable. To forgive means pardoning the unpardonable. Faith means believing the unbelievable. Hope means hoping when everything seems hopeless."

G.K. Chesterton

COME HOLY SPIRIT, RENEW ME, DWELL IN ME AND PROTECT ME

COME HOLY SPIRIT, RENEW ME, DWELL IN ME AND PROTECT ME

COME HOLY SPIRIT, RENEW ME, DWELL IN ME AND PROTECT ME

COME HOLY SPIRIT, RENEW ME, DWELL IN ME AND PROTECT ME

COME HOLY SPIRIT, RENEW ME, DWELL IN ME AND PROTECT ME

COME HOLY SPIRIT, RENEW ME, DWELL IN ME AND PROTECT ME

"Jesus loves hidden souls. A hidden flower is the most fragrant. I must strive to make the interior of my soul a resting place for the Heart of Jesus."

Maria Faustina Kowalska

COME HOLY SPIRIT, RENEW ME, DWELL IN ME AND PROTECT ME

COME HOLY SPIRIT, RENEW ME, DWELL IN ME AND PROTECT ME

COME HOLY SPIRIT, RENEW ME, DWELL IN ME AND PROTECT ME

COME HOLY SPIRIT, RENEW ME, DWELL IN ME AND PROTECT ME

COME HOLY SPIRIT, RENEW ME, DWELL IN ME AND PROTECT ME

COME HOLY SPIRIT, RENEW ME, DWELL IN ME AND PROTECT ME

"If there were no God,
there would be no atheists."

G.K. Chesterton

COME HOLY SPIRIT, RENEW ME, DWELL IN ME AND PROTECT ME

COME HOLY SPIRIT, RENEW ME, DWELL IN ME AND PROTECT ME

COME HOLY SPIRIT, RENEW ME, DWELL IN ME AND PROTECT ME

COME HOLY SPIRIT, RENEW ME, DWELL IN ME AND PROTECT ME

COME HOLY SPIRIT, RENEW ME, DWELL IN ME AND PROTECT ME

COME HOLY SPIRIT, RENEW ME, DWELL IN ME AND PROTECT ME

COME HOLY SPIRIT, RENEW ME, DWELL IN ME AND PROTECT ME

If you are what you should be, you will set the whole world ablaze!

St. Catherine of Sienna

COME HOLY SPIRIT, RENEW ME, DWELL IN ME AND PROTECT ME

COME HOLY SPIRIT, RENEW ME, DWELL IN ME AND PROTECT ME

COME HOLY SPIRIT, RENEW ME, DWELL IN ME AND PROTECT ME

COME HOLY SPIRIT, RENEW ME, DWELL IN ME AND PROTECT ME

COME HOLY SPIRIT, RENEW ME, DWELL IN ME AND PROTECT ME

COME HOLY SPIRIT, RENEW ME, DWELL IN ME AND PROTECT ME

"The most deadly poison of our times is indifference. And this happens, although the praise of God should know no limits. Let us strive, therefore, to praise him to the greatest extent of our powers."

<u>Maximilian Kolbe</u>

COME HOLY SPIRIT, RENEW ME, DWELL IN ME AND PROTECT ME

COME HOLY SPIRIT, RENEW ME, DWELL IN ME AND PROTECT ME

COME HOLY SPIRIT, RENEW ME, DWELL IN ME AND PROTECT ME

COME HOLY SPIRIT, RENEW ME, DWELL IN ME AND PROTECT ME

COME HOLY SPIRIT, RENEW ME, DWELL IN ME AND PROTECT ME

"Fairy tales are more than true —
not because they tell us dragons
exist, but because they tell us
dragons can be beaten."
G.K. Chesterton

COME HOLY SPIRIT, RENEW ME, DWELL IN ME AND PROTECT ME

COME HOLY SPIRIT, RENEW ME, DWELL IN ME AND PROTECT ME

COME HOLY SPIRIT, RENEW ME, DWELL IN ME AND PROTECT ME

COME HOLY SPIRIT, RENEW ME, DWELL IN ME AND PROTECT ME

COME HOLY SPIRIT, RENEW ME, DWELL IN ME AND PROTECT ME

COME HOLY SPIRIT, RENEW ME, DWELL IN ME AND PROTECT ME

"The struggle is the sign of holiness.
A Saint is a sinner that keeps trying"

St Josemaria Escriva

COME HOLY SPIRIT, RENEW ME, DWELL IN ME AND PROTECT ME

COME HOLY SPIRIT, RENEW ME, DWELL IN ME AND PROTECT ME

COME HOLY SPIRIT, RENEW ME, DWELL IN ME AND PROTECT ME

COME HOLY SPIRIT, RENEW ME, DWELL IN ME AND PROTECT ME

COME HOLY SPIRIT, RENEW ME, DWELL IN ME AND PROTECT ME

COME HOLY SPIRIT, RENEW ME, DWELL IN ME AND PROTECT ME

"It was pride that changed angels into devils; it is humility that makes men as angels."

Saint Augustine

COME HOLY SPIRIT, RENEW ME, DWELL IN ME AND PROTECT ME

COME HOLY SPIRIT, RENEW ME, DWELL IN ME AND PROTECT ME

COME HOLY SPIRIT, RENEW ME, DWELL IN ME AND PROTECT ME

COME HOLY SPIRIT, RENEW ME, DWELL IN ME AND PROTECT ME

You cannot be half a saint;
you must be a whole saint or no
saint at all.

St. Therese of Lisieux

COME HOLY SPIRIT, RENEW ME, DWELL IN ME AND PROTECT ME

COME HOLY SPIRIT, RENEW ME, DWELL IN ME AND PROTECT ME

COME HOLY SPIRIT, RENEW ME, DWELL IN ME AND PROTECT ME

COME HOLY SPIRIT, RENEW ME, DWELL IN ME AND PROTECT ME

COME HOLY SPIRIT, RENEW ME, DWELL IN ME AND PROTECT ME

Faith means battles; if there are no contests, it is because there are none who desire to contend.

St. Ambrose

COME HOLY SPIRIT, RENEW ME, DWELL IN ME AND PROTECT ME

COME HOLY SPIRIT, RENEW ME, DWELL IN ME AND PROTECT ME

COME HOLY SPIRIT, RENEW ME, DWELL IN ME AND PROTECT ME

COME HOLY SPIRIT, RENEW ME, DWELL IN ME AND PROTECT ME

COME HOLY SPIRIT, RENEW ME, DWELL IN ME AND PROTECT ME

COME HOLY SPIRIT, RENEW ME, DWELL IN ME AND PROTECT ME

COME HOLY SPIRIT, RENEW ME, DWELL IN ME AND PROTECT ME

The Bible tells us to love our neighbors, and also to love our enemies; probably because they are generally the same people.

G.K. Chesterton

COME HOLY SPIRIT, RENEW ME, DWELL IN ME AND PROTECT ME

COME HOLY SPIRIT, RENEW ME, DWELL IN ME AND PROTECT ME

COME HOLY SPIRIT, RENEW ME, DWELL IN ME AND PROTECT ME

COME HOLY SPIRIT, RENEW ME, DWELL IN ME AND PROTECT ME

COME HOLY SPIRIT, RENEW ME, DWELL IN ME AND PROTECT ME

COME HOLY SPIRIT, RENEW ME, DWELL IN ME AND PROTECT ME

"Actions speak louder than words. Let your words teach and your actions speak."
Anthony of Padua

COME HOLY SPIRIT, RENEW ME, DWELL IN ME AND PROTECT ME

COME HOLY SPIRIT, RENEW ME, DWELL IN ME AND PROTECT ME

COME HOLY SPIRIT, RENEW ME, DWELL IN ME AND PROTECT ME

COME HOLY SPIRIT, RENEW ME, DWELL IN ME AND PROTECT ME

Faith does not quench desire, but inflames it.

St. Thomas Aquinas

COME HOLY SPIRIT, RENEW ME, DWELL IN ME AND PROTECT ME

COME HOLY SPIRIT, RENEW ME, DWELL IN ME AND PROTECT ME

COME HOLY SPIRIT, RENEW ME, DWELL IN ME AND PROTECT ME

COME HOLY SPIRIT, RENEW ME, DWELL IN ME AND PROTECT ME

"It has been often said, very truly, that religion is the thing that makes the ordinary man feel extraordinary; it is an equally important truth that religion is the thing that makes the extraordinary man feel ordinary."

G.K. Chesterton

COME HOLY SPIRIT, RENEW ME, DWELL IN ME AND PROTECT ME

COME HOLY SPIRIT, RENEW ME, DWELL IN ME AND PROTECT ME

COME HOLY SPIRIT, RENEW ME, DWELL IN ME AND PROTECT ME

COME HOLY SPIRIT, RENEW ME, DWELL IN ME AND PROTECT ME

God gives each one of us sufficient grace ever to know His holy will, and to do it fully.

St. Ignatius of Loyola

COME HOLY SPIRIT, RENEW ME, DWELL IN ME AND PROTECT ME

COME HOLY SPIRIT, RENEW ME, DWELL IN ME AND PROTECT ME

COME HOLY SPIRIT, RENEW ME, DWELL IN ME AND PROTECT ME

COME HOLY SPIRIT, RENEW ME, DWELL IN ME AND PROTECT ME

COME HOLY SPIRIT, RENEW ME, DWELL IN ME AND PROTECT ME

Made in the USA
Middletown, DE
13 January 2020